Cult Sando

This first one's for Mum,
for every meal you put on the table.
Thank you x

Cult Sando

カルトサンド

Classic and modern recipes
for the popular Japanese sandwich

Jimmy Callaway

Hardie Grant

BOOKS

Contents

Introduction

In Japan, sando are everywhere: on convenience store shelves, Shinkansen (bullet train) menus and even in vending machines. Their rising popularity in the West over the past decade means sando now appear on the menus of high-end restaurants and hipster pop-ups everywhere. But what is it about these unassuming, typically crustless sandwiches that has garnered such a cult following?

Sando falls into the culinary food group of *yōshoku* (洋食), which roughly translates as 'Western food'. These are Japanese versions of popular dishes and include *karēraisu* (curry rice, a Japanese interpretation of classic curry), *hambagu* (hamburger or beef patty), *omurice* (fried rice encased in an omelette) and *korokke* (a take on the French croquette).

Perhaps the popularity of sando is due to their seemingly simple design. As with all great inventions, however, sando are not always as they seem. They are a culinary example of the Japanese pursuit of perfection, but what makes sando unique among sandwiches is that they are wrapped and pressed. This unites the filling and bread so that, when cut, they make a beautiful cross-section. They are usually served chilled or at room temperature, but almost never hot, even with a katsu filling.

The bread used in sando is called *shokupan* (食パン). This sweet, light milk bread is as ubiquitous in Japan as katsu, gyoza, udon and ramen. Bread in Japan can be dated back to the 16th-century trade with Portuguese missionaries. When Christianity was banned in the 19th-century Edo period, any form of bread went with it. Bread made a comeback to the Japanese diet with the advent of World War II. Similarly to the rest of the world, Japan faced enormous food shortages, even with German-delivered wheat. Made from milk, yeast, butter, sugar, salt and wheat flour, shokupan was allegedly first baked by Japanese soldiers using nothing but a baking tin, jumper leads and the battery from a tank! Fast forward to the 1970s, when Japan eagerly embraced bread culture, and the sando was born.

From Japanese classics such as egg salad and pork katsu to recipes with more contemporary fillings, such as mortadella, tofu and ice cream, you're bound to stumble upon your next *Cult Sando* within the pages of this book.

Japanese Ingredients

日本の食材

AMAEBI PRAWNS (SHRIMP)
These 'sweet prawns' are native to the cold waters of northern Japan and Russia. They are prized for their sweetness and are preferably eaten raw or barely cooked.

BONITO FLAKES Also known as *katsuobushi* or *okaka*, these fine shavings of dried skipjack tuna fillet are one of the hero ingredients in *dashi kombu*, the base broth for many Japanese dishes.

DASHI KOMBU A base stock made from *kombu* (dried kelp), bonito flakes and water. It is always best to make this aromatic stock from scratch. Avoid the pre-packaged stuff — it doesn't compare in flavour.

FURIKAKE A sprinkle seasoning for rice and, in some cases, protein. It comes in a plethora of combinations. Said to be more than 900 years old, modern *furikake* was invented in the Taishō Era (1912–1926).

JAPANESE CURRY MIX A roux-thickened curry sauce adapted to the Japanese palate. Introduced in the Meiji Era (1868–1912) when the Asian subcontinent was under British rule, *karē* (curry) is a long-standing member of yōshoku in Japan.

JAPANESE MAYO The secret to the complex taste of Japanese mayo is that it uses a blend of vinegars, such as rice vinegar, apple cider vinegar and red wine vinegar. It's made using egg yolks, which give it a thick, creamy texture.

KARASHI MUSTARD Hot, slightly bitter and with a distinctive horseradish taste, *karashi* is made by crushing brown mustard seeds (*Brassica juncea*). You can use it as a pickling agent, filling or condiment.

KOMBU A dried brown kelp, umami-rich kombu is not to be confused with nori (which is thinner and shredded). When buying, look for minimal breakages, and a product that is kelp only, with no added ingredients.

NAMA PANKO Freshly torn breadcrumbs commonly made from shokupan, these are two or three times larger than dried panko. When fried, nama panko create an intensely crisp and light crumb. See page 12 for how to make these breadcrumbs.

NORI This dried red algae is made by shredding seaweed and pressing it into thin sheets, in a process similar to that of making paper. Coming in many varieties, nori also has health benefits, with 10 times more calcium than milk!

SHICHIMI TŌGARASHI Commonly known as seven spice, *tōgarashi* is Japanese for 'red pepper' (*Capsicum annuum*), which gives this mix its spicy character. A recipe for this spice mix can be found on page 97.

SHIRO MISO Made by fermenting soybeans and rice, *shiro* miso is typically aged for a shorter period than the darker miso varieties *shinshu* (yellow) and *aka* (red). It has a salty, sweet richness that's slightly toasted and deeply savoury. Shiro miso also works brilliantly in desserts.

SHISO (PERILLA) LEAF A herb in the mint family (*Lamiaceae*), that tastes of mint, tarragon, basil, cinnamon and anise. It pairs well with fatty fish, such as tuna and salmon, and even some fruits and vegetables.

SHOKUPAN Otherwise known as milk bread, this bread is unique for the process by which it's made. You start with a *tangzhong* (similar to a roux) that you add to the dough, which helps to retain the lightness and moisture once baked. Shokupan is available to purchase from most Japanese or Asian grocers, but if your local store doesn't stock it, then thick-cut white bread is a great alternative.

SHOYU Essentially Japanese soy sauce, it can be dark (*koikuchi*) or light (*usukuchi*). Shoyu originated in the Kensi region in about 1580, during the Tenso Era.

TONKATSU SAUCE A blend of stewed fruits and vegetables seasoned with salt, sugar and vinegars. *Tonkatsu* sauce was adapted from yōshoku cuisine, and dates back to the 1930s. A recipe for this sauce can be found on page 102.

TSUYU SAUCE Otherwise known as *mentsuyu*, this is a rich, slightly smoky dipping sauce that's similar to soy. It can be thinned out with water and is most often used for tempura.

YUZU The unique aroma and flavour of this fruit is like the sweetness of mandarin with the perfume of grapefruit. A versatile citrus, it works just as well with fish and protein as it does with delicate pastry.

YUZU KOSHO Made by fermenting the juice and zest of yuzu with bird's eye chillies and salt for up to a week, this heady and pungent condiment packs a punch. It's best served sparingly with everything from seared wagyu beef to sashimi.

Suggested Techniques

TECHNIQUE	HOW TO
TOASTED NORI	To toast nori, take one corner of a nori sheet and gently fan over a low to medium flame or charcoal embers until it becomes aromatic and crisp. Do not rush — nori burns quite easily. Use immediately.
NAMA PANKO	These are fresh breadcrumbs that are typically used in the top katsu restaurants in Japan because, once fried, they make an exceptionally crispy coating. To make nama panko, simply remove the crusts from a loaf of shokupan, then shred the remaining bread into bite-sized pieces. If you prefer a finer crumb, place the shredded bread in a food processor and blitz. Store in an airtight container until needed.
SANDO PRESSING	Pressing is an essential part of the sando process. It helps the sando retain its stable structure when sliced. Typically, all sando are pressed, apart from those that might be served hot. To press, wrap the sando in cling film (plastic wrap) and place two plates (1kg/2 lb each) on top. Press for the time specified in the recipe (the time varies depending on the filling).
CRUMBING STATION	To set up a crumbing station, place three deep baking trays (baking sheets) on the bench. The first will contain plain (all-purpose) flour. The second will contain whisked egg. The third will contain panko (fresh or dry panko, depending on the recipe). You can also have another tray next to the panko with a layer of baking (parchment) paper, on to which you can place the crumbed food.
MARKING YOUR CUT	When it comes to cutting your sando, be careful to consider the direction in which you have placed the ingredients, as this will help you to achieve the prettiest cross-section once cut. It can be very helpful to draw a line with a marker once the sando wrapped in cling film, just before it is pressed.

 A NOTE ABOUT MEASUREMENTS In Australia, tablespoons are 20 ml, while in the UK and USA, tablespoons are 15 ml. The recipes in this book use Australian tablespoons.

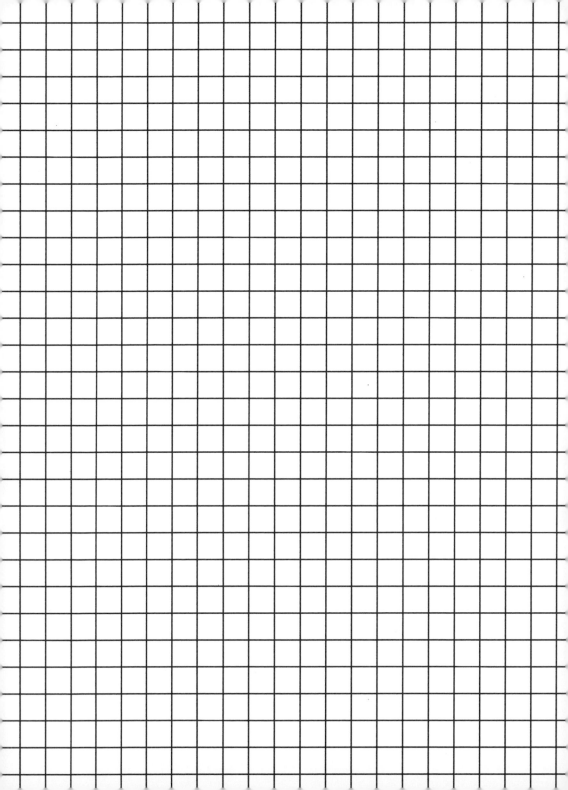

Classics

Egg Salad and Boiled Egg

Second only to pork katsu in the sando hall of fame, this is simply layers and textures of egg dressed in Japanese mayo. If it ain't broke, don't fix it. When pressing the sando, it's important to remember which line you will cut down to show the cross-section of the egg.

Makes 2

6 eggs
1½ tablespoons Japanese mayo
2 teaspoons caster (superfine) sugar
½ teaspoon karashi mustard
pinch of sea salt
2 teaspoons double (heavy) cream
2 tablespoons salted butter
4 slices shokupan

//
PREP/COOK TIME 24 minutes
PRESS TIME 30 minutes

1. Bring a medium-sized pot of water to the boil, then gently add the eggs and boil for 8 minutes. Remove two eggs, and allow the remaining eggs to cook for a further 2 minutes.

2. Cool all the eggs under cold running water and peel (being sure to keep the 8-minute eggs separate).

3. In a medium-sized bowl, combine the mayo, sugar, mustard and salt, then whisk to dissolve the sugar.

4. Cut the 10-minute eggs in half and remove the yolks. Crumble the yolks into the mayo mixture and add the cream, then whisk vigorously to combine.

5. Finely dice the 10-minute egg whites and fold into the mayo mixture.

6. Evenly spread the butter over the four slices of shokupan. Cut the 8-minute eggs in half and place, cut-side down, on two of the slices.

7. Top the egg halves with the mayo mixture, then the remaining shokupan slices, butter-side down.

8. Gently wrap the sando in cling film (plastic wrap) and press for 30 minutes.

9. To serve, trim the crusts and cut widthways.

卵サラダ

Fruit Salad

フルーツサラダ

Iconic, refreshing and perhaps a little strange, the secret to this sando is the quality of the produce set within the decadent filling.

Makes 2

4 tablespoons caster (superfine) sugar
120 ml (4 fl oz/½ cup) whipping (thickened) cream
120 ml (4 fl oz/½ cup) double (heavy) cream
1 teaspoon dark rum
4 slices shokupan
1 kiwi fruit, peeled and quartered lengthways
6 strawberries, hulled
1 orange, peeled and pith removed

//
PREP/COOK TIME 15 minutes
PRESS TIME 20 minutes

1. In a medium-sized bowl, gently whisk the caster sugar into the whipping cream to dissolve. Add the double cream and rum, then whisk until stiff peaks form.

2. Spread ½ tablespoon of the cream mixture onto each slice of shokupan.

3. Over two of the slices, arrange three strawberries in a row in the middle. Place a piece of kiwi in the top right corner and a piece of orange in the bottom left corner.

4. Divide the remaining cream mixture over the fruit, then top with the remaining slices of bread.

5. Gently wrap in cling film (plastic wrap), marking the cross-section line on the film with a marker, and press for 20 minutes in the fridge.

6. To serve, trim the crusts and cut diagonally on the cross-section line.

Classics

Dashimaki Tamagoyaki with Shiso Leaf

シソとだし巻きたまご

As this sando requires making tamagoyaki, a renownedly difficult food to master, the effort required to master this recipe may seem daunting, but rest assured, you'll be rewarded with a tasty, textural delight. Plus, you'll pick up some hardcore sando skills along the way.

Makes 2

4 tablespoons Japanese mayo
4 slices shokupan
4 large shiso (perilla) leaves
2 x 180 g (6¼ oz) dashimaki
   tamagoyaki, cut into 9 x 10 cm
   (3½ x 4 in) pieces (page 90)

//

PREP/COOK TIME 40 minutes
PRESS TIME 30 minutes

1. Evenly spread the Japanese mayo over four slices of shokupan.

2. Lay one large shiso leaf over each slice.

3. Lay the tamagoyaki pieces over the bottom slices. Top with the remaining slices, shiso-side down.

4. Wrap in cling film (plastic wrap) and press for 30 minutes.

5. To serve, trim the crusts and divide in half diagonally.

Classics

Pork Cutlet, Tonkatsu Sauce and White Cabbage

トンカツ

Behold, the most famous katsu of them all! The secret is a triple threat of fatty high-quality pork, nama panko, and a sweet and tangy tonkatsu sauce.

Makes 2

1 litre (34 fl oz/4 cups) rapeseed (canola) oil, for frying
150 g (5 oz/1¼ cups) plain (all-purpose) flour
3 eggs, whisked
250 g (9 oz/4 cups) nama panko (page 12)
2 x 180 g (6¼ oz) pork cutlets, sliced 2 cm (¾ in) thick, then cut into 10 x 10 cm (4 x 4 in) pieces
100 ml (3½ fl oz) Tonkatsu Sauce (page 102)
80 g (3 oz) salted butter, softened
4 slices shokupan
60 g (2¼ oz) white cabbage, finely shredded

1. Put the oil in a deep-fryer and set to 90°C (195°F).

2. Set up a crumbing station (page 12): in three consecutive trays, place the plain flour first, eggs second and nama panko third.

3. With a skewer, thoroughly prick the surface of the pork.

4. Lightly dust the pork on all sides with the flour, shaking to remove any excess. Coat in the egg-wash. Repeat the flour and egg-wash, then finish by covering thoroughly with nama panko.

5. Gently place the pork katsu in the deep-fryer for 4 minutes (the crumb should be light blonde in colour). Remove from the fryer and place on a wire rack. Set the fryer to 170°C (340°F). Once at temperature, fry the katsu for a further 1 minute until golden brown and very crispy.

6. Place on a wire rack, standing upright, to drain for 6 minutes. Once rested, lay flat and drizzle half the tonkatsu sauce over the two pieces.

7. Evenly spread the butter across four slices of shokupan. Divide the shredded cabbage across two slices of the bread.

8. Lay the pork katsu pieces on the cabbage, sauce-side down, and drizzle over the remaining tonkatsu sauce. Top with the remaining slices of shokupan.

9. Wrap in cling film (plastic wrap) and press for 15 minutes.

10. To serve, trim the crusts and cut into thirds widthways.

//

PREP/COOK TIME 40 minutes
PRESS TIME 15 minutes

Kobe Beef with Tonkatsu Sauce and Yuzu Kosho

This is the 'banker's lunch' in sando form. Irresistibly crispy, this rich Kobe beef katsu is anything but excessive when combined with the spicy and floral citrus notes of yuzu kosho.

Makes 2

3 litres (104 fl oz/12 cups) rapeseed (canola) oil, for frying
4 tablespoons Japanese mayo
1 tablespoon yuzu kosho
60 g (2¼ oz/½ cup) plain (all-purpose) flour
1 egg, whisked
250 g (9 oz/4 cups) nama panko (page 12)
2 x 210 g (7½ oz) Kobe sirloin steaks, sliced 2.5 cm (1 in thick), then cut into 9.5 x 9.5 cm (3¾ x 3¾ in) pieces
4 slices shokupan
125 ml (4 fl oz/½ cup) Tonkatsu Sauce (page 102)
salt and pepper to taste

//
PREP/COOK TIME 35 minutes
PRESS TIME 15 minutes

1. Put the oil in a deep-fryer and set to 170°C (340°F).

2. Whisk together the mayo and yuzu kosho and set aside.

3. Set up a crumbing station (page 12): in three consecutive trays, place the plain flour first, egg second and nama panko third.

4. Lightly dust both pieces of sirloin with plain flour, shaking off excess. Dip in egg-wash and thoroughly coat in nama panko, leaving no exposed areas. Rest in crumbs for 5 minutes.

5. Gently place the sirloin in a deep-fryer and cook for 3 minutes. Look for an internal temperature of 40°C (105°F): the crumb should be a golden-amber colour.

6. Once ready, remove from the fryer and rest upright on a wire rack for 4 minutes. Season to taste.

7. Evenly spread the yuzu kosho mixture over four slices of shokupan. Once the Kobe katsu has rested, drizzle half the tonkatsu sauce over the katsu and place on two of the slices of bread.

8. Pour over the remaining tonkatsu sauce and top with the remaining shokupan slices. Wrap in cling film (plastic wrap) and press for 15 minutes.

9. To serve, trim the crusts and cut into six square pieces.

神戸牛カツとゆず胡椒

Ebi Katsu

エビフライ

With juicy fried prawns (shrimp) in a curry-powder mayo, this sando has its very own cult following. Make it and you'll soon see why! *Hanpen* fish cakes are a soft, square shape found at most Japanese grocers, but a regular fish ball will work just as well here.

Makes 2

3 litres (104 fl oz/12 cups)
  rapeseed (canola) oil, for frying
200 g (7 oz) medium-sized prawns
  (shrimp), peeled and deveined
50 g (1¾ oz) hanpen fish cakes,
  or 4 fish balls
½ teaspoon cornflour
  (cornstarch)
salt and pepper
60 g (2¼ oz/½ cup) plain
  (all-purpose) flour
1 egg, whisked
100 g (3½ oz/1½ cups) nama
  panko (page 12)
2 tablespoons Japanese mayo
1 teaspoon curry powder
1 teaspoon tomato ketchup
4 slices shokupan

1. Put the oil in a deep-fryer, then set to 170°C (340°F).

2. Place six prawns, all the fish cakes and the cornflour into a small high-speed food processor. Blend into a smooth paste.

3. Combine the prawn mixture and the remaining prawns in a bowl and season with a pinch of salt and pepper. Divide the mixture into two and, with wet hands, form into patties the same size as the shokupan.

4. Set up a crumbing station (page 12): in three consecutive trays, place the plain flour first, egg second and nama panko third.

5. Lightly dust the patties in plain flour, shaking off the excess. Place in the egg-wash, then cover thoroughly with nama panko.

6. Lower the patties into the fryer and cook for 3 minutes, turning every minute. Remove and rest upright on a wire rack for 8 minutes.

7. While resting, combine the mayo, curry powder and ketchup in a small bowl. Evenly spread this mixture over four slices of shokupan.

8. Place the prawn katsu over two of the slices and top with the remaining slices, mayo-side down. Wrap in cling film (plastic wrap) and press for 15 minutes.

9. To serve, trim the crusts and cut in half widthways.

//

PREP/COOK TIME 40 minutes
PRESS TIME 15 minutes

Classics

Ham, Mayo and Cucumber

Simple and unpretentious, yet tasty and reliable. This little guy isn't your craziest friend, but you know he'll pick you up if you need a lift home at 2 am. Two thumbs up.

Makes 2

6 tablespoons Japanese mayo
4 slices shokupan
1 small Lebanese cucumber, cut lengthways into 8 slices
salt and pepper
120 g (4¼ oz) ham, thinly sliced

//
PREP/COOK TIME 10 minutes
PRESS TIME 20 minutes

1. Spread 4 tablespoons of the mayo over four slices of shokupan.

2. Lay the cucumber horizontally on two of the shokupan slices. Season with salt and pepper to taste. Cover the cucumber with the remaining 2 tablespoons mayo.

3. Layer the ham over the cucumber and mayo, then top with the remaining shokupan slices, mayo-side down.

4. Wrap in cling film (plastic wrap) and press for 20 minutes.

5. To serve, trim the crusts and cut in half horizontally.

ハムマヨキュウリ

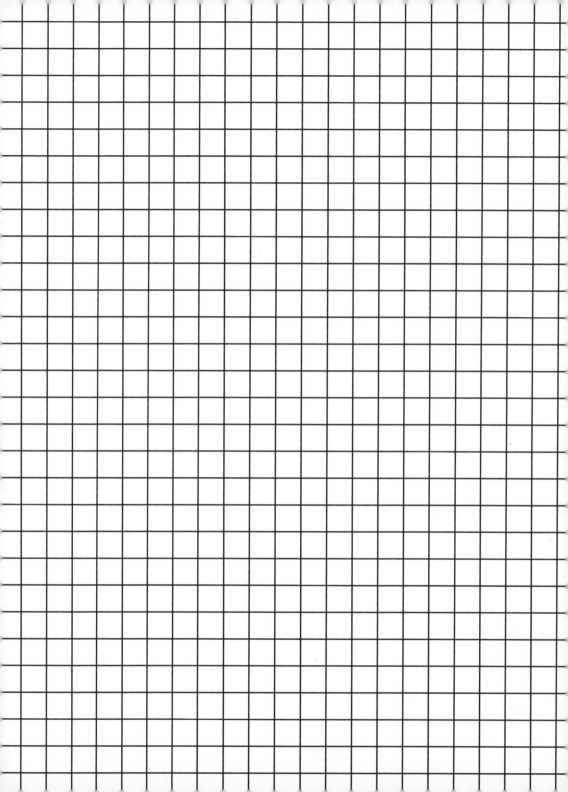

Vegetable

Cucumber, Avocado and Wasabi Cream Cheese

キュウリとアボカドとわさびのクリームチーズ

This fresh green sando could happily hold court at the table of any Japanese high tea, with its layered cucumber and smooth avocado encased in a punchy wasabi cream.

Makes 2

½ portion Wasabi Cream Cheese
  (page 104)
4 slices shokupan
1 avocado, peeled, sliced 1 cm
  (½ in) thick
1 Lebanese cucumber, sliced 1 cm
  (½ in) thick

//

PREP/COOK TIME 10 minutes
PRESS TIME 20 minutes

1. Spread the wasabi cream cheese over four slices of shokupan.

2. On two of the slices, layer the avocado from top to bottom like fallen dominos, followed by two flat layers of cucumber slices placed horizontally. Top with the remaining shokupan slices, wasabi cream-side down.

3. Wrap in cling film (plastic wrap) and press for 20 minutes.

4. To serve, trim the crusts and cut each sando widthways.

Vegetable

Nasu Dengaku

As timeless as strawberries and cream, aubergine (eggplant) and miso are a match made in heaven. Salty, fermented deliciousness.

 Makes 2

60 ml (2 fl oz) vegetable oil
2 x 3 cm (1¼ in) slices aubergine (eggplant), trimmed to the same size as the shokupan
1 portion Miso Glaze (page 93)
½ portion Miso Butter (page 92)
4 slices shokupan

//

PREP/COOK TIME 30 minutes
PRESS TIME 30 minutes

1. Preheat the grill (broiler) to 200°C (450°F) and line a baking tray (baking sheet) with baking (parchment) paper.

2. Heat the oil in a pan over a medium–high heat.

3. Once hot and gently smoking, add the aubergine slices and shallow-fry for about 8 minutes until golden brown.

4. Using a fork, vigorously prick the surface of the aubergine slices and smear over the miso glaze.

5. Place under the grill for 3 minutes, then remove and cool to room temperature.

6. To assemble, spread the miso butter on four slices of shokupan. Lay half a piece of toasted nori on two of the shokupan slices. Place the aubergine on the nori. Top the with remaining slices of shokupan, miso butter-side down.

7. Wrap in cling film (plastic wrap) and press for 30 minutes.

8. To serve, trim the crusts and cut lengthways.

なす田楽

ズッキーニと人参の天ぷら

Placing something as pure as tempura in a sando may seem sacrilegious, but its super-crisp texture against the cloud-like shokupan is a winning combination.

Makes 2

3 litres (104 fl oz/12 cups) rapeseed (canola) oil, for frying
4 baby carrots, washed and trimmed
4 baby courgettes (zucchini), washed and trimmed
150 g (5 oz/1¼) plain (all-purpose) flour
1 portion Tempura Batter (page 100)
2 tablespoons salted butter, softened
4 slices shokupan
4 shiso (perilla) leaves
Tentsuyu (tempura dipping sauce) (page 100), to serve

//

PREP/COOK TIME 20 minutes
PRESS TIME 30 minutes

1. Put the oil in a deep-fryer set to 170°C (340°F). Have a drying rack ready to allow excess oil to drain from the vegetables.

2. Lightly dust the carrots and courgettes in flour and tap off the excess. Dip in the tempura batter, then gently place in the deep-fryer. Cook for 3 minutes.

3. Take 2 tablespoons of the tempura batter and drizzle it into the oil. This will create the *tenkasu* (crispy fried batter).

4. When the vegetables and tenkasu are ready, remove from the oil using a fine sieve and drain on the rack or kitchen paper.

5. Spread the butter over four slices of shokupan. Top each slice with a shiso leaf the same size as the shokupan slices.

6. Place a fine layer of tenkasu on two of the shokupan slices, then top with alternating pieces of tempura carrot and courgette. Top with the remaining shokupan slices, leaf-side down. Wrap in cling film (plastic wrap) and press for 30 minutes.

7. To serve, trim the crusts, cut lengthways and dip in the sauce as desired.

Vegetable

Japanese Potato Salad with Tenderstem Broccoli

This *konbini* (convenience store) hall-of-famer pairs a creamy, almost-sweet mayo with a variety of vegetables. Healthy AND tasty!

ポテトサラダ

Makes 2

¼ white onion, finely diced
¼ carrot, peeled and thinly sliced
5 small new potatoes, peeled and boiled
1 hardboiled egg, diced
60 ml (2 fl oz) Japanese mayo
1 tablespoon rice vinegar
pinch of ground white pepper
4 slices shokupan
6 stalks Tenderstem broccoli, blanched, refreshed and halved

//
PREP/COOK TIME 25 minutes
PRESS TIME 20 minutes

1. Soak the diced onion in warm water for 10 minutes, then strain and pat dry.

2. Place the sliced carrot in a microwave-proof bowl with 1 tablespoon of water and microwave on high for 2 minutes.

3. Roughly mash the potatoes with a fork, then add the diced egg, mayo, soaked onion, carrot and rice vinegar. Stir to combine and season to taste with pepper.

4. Evenly distribute the potato salad across four slices of shokupan. Lay the broccoli horizontally across two of the slices, then top with the other two slices, potato salad-side down.

5. Wrap in cling film (plastic wrap) and press for 20 minutes.

6. To serve, cut horizontally.

Agedashi Tofu with Tsuyu Sauce

揚げだし豆腐

Based on the popular starter, this surprisingly satisfying sando reworks the traditional flavour combination of salty soy and smoky, savoury bonito flakes.

Makes 2

300 g (10½ oz) silken tofu
3 litres (104 fl oz/12 cups)
   rapeseed (canola) oil, for frying
380 g (13 oz/2 cups) potato
   starch
2 portions Tsuyu Glaze
   (page 103)
4 slices shokupan
50 g (1¾ oz) daikon, peeled and
   coarsely grated
1 spring onion (scallion), finely
   diced
1 packet (2 g) bonito flakes

//

PREP/COOK TIME 20 minutes
PRESS TIME 20 minutes

1. Cut lengthways and place between kitchen paper to drain for 15 minutes.

2. Put the oil in a deep-fryer and set to 175°C (345°F).

3. Meanwhile, place the potato starch on a plate. Once the tofu is dry, gently dust it with the potato starch. Deep-fry for about 3 minutes until crispy. Place on a wire rack to allow any excess oil to drain.

4. To assemble, spread 1 tablespoon of the tsuyu glaze evenly across two slices of shokupan. Evenly distribute the daikon over the top, followed by the spring onion. Take the fried tofu pieces and place on top, then drizzle each slice with 1 teaspoon of glaze. Cover with bonito flakes, then top with the remaining slices of shokupan, glaze-side down.

5. Wrap in cling film (plastic wrap) and press for 20 minutes.

6. To serve, trim the crusts and cut lengthways. Garnish with any leftover bonito flakes.

Vegetable Korokke

野菜コロッケ

A Yōshoku interpretation of the French croquette, with finely shredded iceberg lettuce as a textural accompaniment.

Makes 2

3 litres (104 fl oz/12 cups) rapeseed (canola) oil, for frying
280 g (10 oz) potatoes, peeled and chopped into large chunks
2 tablespoons table salt
1 tablespoon vegetable oil
¼ carrot, peeled and cut into 1 cm (½ in) cubes
¼ brown onion, finely diced
40 g (1½ oz/¼ cup) shelled and blanched edamame
salt and pepper
1 egg
60 ml (2 fl oz) Japanese mayo, plus 4 tablespoons
1 tablespoon plain (all-purpose) flour
60 ml (2 fl oz) water
100 g (3½ oz/1½ cups) Nama Panko (page 12)
1 tablespoon karashi mustard
4 slices shokupan
40 g (1½ oz) iceberg lettuce, finely shredded

1. Put the rapeseed oil in a deep-fryer and set to 160°C (320°F).

2. In a medium-sized pot, cover the potatoes with cold water. Add the measured salt and boil for about 25 minutes, until the potatoes are soft. Strain and allow to cool to room temperature.

3. Mash the potatoes with a fork, leaving some chunks for texture.

4. Heat the vegetable oil in a frying pan (skillet) over a medium heat. Once hot, sauté the carrot for 2 minutes, then add the onion and cook for a further 2½ minutes. Transfer to a bowl and allow to cool to room temperature.

5. Add the cooked vegetables and edamame to the potato mixture, then season to taste and divide into two patties, about 10 x 9 cm (4 x 3½ in) each.

6. Make the batter by adding the egg, Japanese mayo, flour and water to a bowl and mixing to combine.

7. Add one patty to the batter, ensuring it's fully coated. Cover in nama panko and fry for 5 minutes. Repeat with the second patty.

8. In a bowl, mix together the 4 tablespoons of Japanese mayo and the mustard. Spread the mustard mayo evenly across four slices of shokupan.

9. Place the iceberg lettuce on two slices of the bread, followed by the korokke. Top with the remaining shokupan slices, mayo-side down.

10. Wrap in cling film (plastic wrap) and press for 15 minutes.

11. To serve, trim the crusts and cut in half widthways.

//

PREP/COOK TIME 35 minutes
PRESS TIME 6 minutes, then flip and press for a further 6 minutes

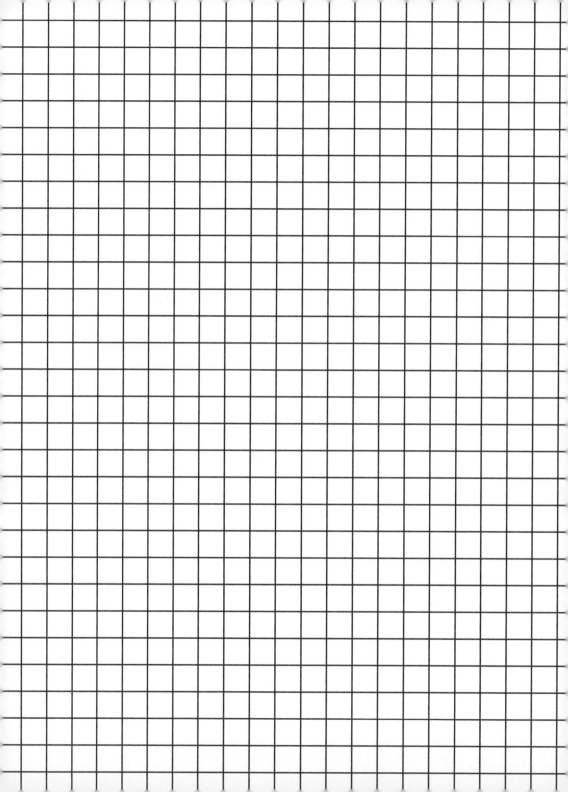

Seafood

Ponzu Tuna with Daikon and Furikake

ぽん酢和えまぐろと大根とふりかけ

This is my adaptation of a friend's recipe. The umami of the fried nori, the peppery crunch of daikon and the salty citrus notes of ponzu butter are the perfect support act for a cut of tuna sashimi.

Makes 2

2 x 160 g (5¾ oz) pieces sashimi grade tuna, sliced 2–2.5 cm (¾–1 in) thick, then cut into 9 x 9 cm (3½ x 3½ in) pieces
600 ml (20 fl oz/2½ cups) Ponzu (page 94)
50 g (1¾ oz/½ cup) furikake nori fumi seasoning
100 ml (3½ fl oz) vegetable oil
1 portion Ponzu Butter (page 94)
4 slices shokupan
120 g (4¼ oz) daikon, thinly sliced into 8 cm (3 in) long pieces

1. Put the tuna and ponzu in a container large enough to submerge both pieces of fish, then leave in the fridge to marinate for 4 hours.

2. Once marinated, remove the tuna from the ponzu and lightly pat dry. Discard the ponzu. Cover the tuna in furikake. Press lightly on all sides to ensure even coverage.

3. Heat the vegetable oil in a medium-sized saucepan over a medium heat until lightly smoking. Dust any excess furikake off the tuna and gently place in the pan. Sear for 30 seconds on each side. Remove the tuna from the pan and allow to cool to room temperature.

4. Evenly distribute the ponzu butter across four slices of shokupan.

5. Lay the daikon slices horizontally over each piece of bread (you will be cutting down this line). Place the tuna pieces on two of the shokupan slices and top with the remaining slices, daikon-side down.

6. Wrap in cling film (plastic wrap) and press for 10 minutes. Meanwhile, turn the grill (broiler) to high.

7. Once pressed, unwrap the sando and place on a baking tray (baking sheet) lined with baking (parchment) paper. Grill (broil) on both sides until golden brown.

8. To serve, trim the crusts and cut widthways.

//

MARINATING TIME 4 hours
PREP/COOK TIME 30 minutes
PRESS TIME 10 minutes

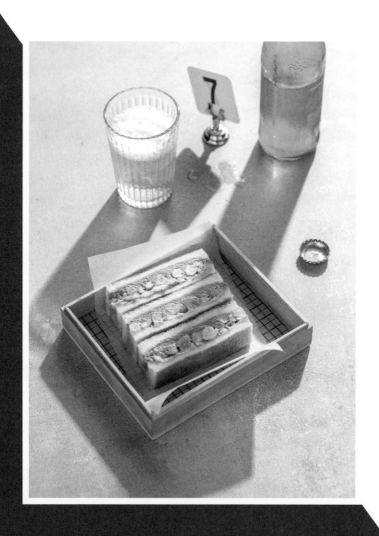

Amaebi Prawn and Pâté

This unusual but delicious combination is brought together by an indulgent pâté, which makes these sashimi prawns (shrimps) dressed in roasted prawn oil really sing.

Makes 2

240 g (8½ oz) sashimi-grade
  amaebi prawns (shrimp)
125 ml (4 fl oz/½ cup) Roasted
  Prawn Oil (page 96)
2 tablespoons Chicken Liver Pâté
  (page 88)
4 slices shokupan

//

MARINATING TIME 2 hours
PREP/COOK TIME 40 minutes
PRESS TIME 20 minutes

1. Combine the peeled prawns and prawn oil in a container. Gently stir, then wrap with cling film (plastic wrap) and allow to marinate in the fridge for 2 hours.

2. After 2 hours, evenly distribute the pâté across four slices of shokupan.

3. Strain the prawns, leaving a thin coating of prawn oil. Evenly distribute the prawns between two slices of shokupan. Top with the remaining slices.

4. Wrap in cling film and press for 20 minutes. Meanwhile, preheat the grill (broiler) to high.

5. Once pressed, toast both sides of the sando under the grill until golden brown.

6. To serve, trim the crusts and cut widthways.

甘エビのパルフェ

Curried Lobster

カレー風味のロブスター

Enjoying lobster and silky layers of curried egg with a daring amount of butter on toasted shokupan tastes and feels like you're at the pointy end of the plane.

Makes 2

160 ml (5¼ fl oz/⅔ cup) water
30 g (1 oz) block hot Japanese curry mix
4 eggs
400 g (14 oz) lobster tail meat, cut into 3 cm (1¼ in) cubes
2 tablespoons vegetable oil
4 tablespoons unsalted butter
4 slices shokupan

1. Heat the water in a small pan over a medium heat. Break up the Japanese curry block and whisk it into the water until completely dissolved. Cook for 3 minutes.

2. Once cooked, remove from the heat and allow to cool.

3. Whisk the eggs with two chopsticks, then add the curry mixture and whisk until completely combined (but not a foam).

4. Add the lobster meat and stir gently to combine.

5. Prepare the lobster in two even batches.* First, heat 1 tablespoon of the vegetable oil in a medium-sized non-stick pan over a medium heat. Once lightly smoking, pour in half of the lobster mixture.

6. Gently move the lobster mixture around on the heat for 10 seconds. Take off the heat. Form the mixture into a 9 cm (3½ in) square. Allow to cook in the residual heat for a further 90 seconds without moving.

7. Evenly spread the butter over four slices of shokupan. Remove the cooked lobster mixture from the pan and place onto a slice of shokupan. Top with a second slice, butter-side down.

8. Repeat this process with the remaining lobster mixture to make a second sando.

9. Wrap the sando in cling film (plastic wrap) and press for 3 minutes. Turn the grill (broiler) to high and toast the sando until golden brown on both sides.

10. To serve, trim the crusts and cut in half lengthways.

* Tip: The best way to divide the lobster is to weigh the total mixture, then divide by two and split into two bowls.

//
PREP/COOK TIME 35 minutes
PRESS TIME 3 minutes

Hokkaido Scallop Katsu and Green Onion Nori

北海道ホタテカツとネギのり

A sando of individually fried scallop katsu nestled in aromatic fried spring onion, sesame oil and nori mayo.

Makes 2

3 litres (104 fl oz/12 cups) rapeseed (canola) oil, for frying
2 tablespoons sesame oil
2 spring onions (scallions), green parts only, finely diced
100 g (3½ oz/2 cups) dried panko crumbs
2 tablespoons rice flour
150 g (5 oz/1¼ cup) plain (all-purpose) flour
2 eggs, whisked
8 large whole scallops, cleaned and dried between kitchen paper for 6 hours in the fridge
4 tablespoons Toasted Nori Mayo (page 101)
4 slices shokupan

//

PREP/COOK TIME 40 minutes
PRESS TIME 3 minutes

1. Put the rapeseed oil in a deep-fryer and set to 180°C (350°F).

2. Heat the sesame oil in a small saucepan over a medium heat for 1 minute. Add the spring onions and stir for 20 seconds. Remove from the heat and allow to cool.

3. Combine the panko and rice flour. Set up a crumbing station (page 12): in three consecutive trays, place the plain flour first, eggs second and panko mixture third.

4. Remove the scallops from fridge and roll in the plain flour, followed by egg-wash and then the panko mixture. Allow to sit in the panko mixture for 4 minutes, ensuring each scallop is completely covered.

5. Remove the scallops from the panko and gently place in the deep-fryer. Cook for about 1 minutes until golden brown, then remove and drain on kitchen paper.

6. Evenly spread the nori mayo on two slices of shokupan. Place the spring onions, followed by the scallops, on the remaining slices.

7. Top with the remaining shokupan slices, nori mayo-side down.

8. Wrap in cling film (plastic wrap) and press for 3 minutes. To serve, trim the crusts and cut in thirds widthways.

Seafood

Swordfish Katsu with Shichimi Tonkatsu Sauce

This simple and neat swordfish sando may look understated, but it will leave you returning for another fierce, fiery mouthful.

Makes 2

1 litre (34 fl oz/4 cups) rapeseed (canola) oil, for frying
75 g (2½ oz/½ cup) plain (all-purpose) flour
2 eggs, whisked
100 g (3½ oz/2 cups) nama panko
125 ml (4 fl oz/½ cup) Tonkatsu Sauce (page 102)
25 g (1 oz/¼ cup) Shichimi Togarashi (page 97)
2 x 200 g (7 oz) swordfish cutlets, cut into 9 x 12 cm (3½ x 4½ in) pieces, skin and bloodline removed
2 tablespoons salted butter, softened
4 slices shokupan

//

PREP/COOK TIME 30 minutes
PRESS TIME 5 minutes

1. Place the oil in the deep-fryer and set to 190°C (375°F).

2. Set up a crumbing station (page 12): in three consecutive trays, place the plain flour first, eggs second and panko third.

3. In a small bowl, combine the tonkatsu sauce and shichimi togarashi and set aside.

4. Dust the swordfish cutlets in flour, shake off any excess, then dip in the egg-wash followed by the panko. Cover thoroughly.

5. Gently place both cutlets in the fryer and fry for about 1 minutes until golden brown.

6. Remove from the fryer and allow to drain on a wire rack for about 3 minutes.

7. Evenly butter four slices of shokupan. Lightly dip both sides of the swordfish cutlets into the tonkatsu mixture. Place on two of the shokupan slices and top with the remaining slices.

8. Press unwrapped (between two pieces of baking/parchment paper) for 5 minutes.

9. To serve, trim the crusts and cut widthways.

カジキフライ 七味トンカツソース

King Crab, Avocado and Cucumber

タラバガニとアボカドとキュウリ

Finally — crab and avocado restored to its former 1970s glory! In this recipe for the ages, king crab, with its delicately tender and sweet meat, is matched with cucumber, lime and avocado.

Makes 2

1 avocado
2 tablespoons lemon juice
½ teaspoon sea salt flakes
6 tablespoons Japanese mayo
4 slices shokupan
260 g (9¼ oz) king crab leg meat
1 small Lebanese cucumber,
    de-seeded and finely diced

//

PREP/COOK TIME 20 minutes
PRESS TIME 30 minutes

1. Peel the avocado and place half the flesh in a small bowl with the lemon juice and salt. Mash to a purée.

2. Dice the remaining avocado half into 1 cm (½ in) cubes then add to the mashed avocado mixture. Add the seeded and diced cucumber. Gently stir and set aside.

3. Evenly spread the Japanese mayo over four slices of shokupan.

4. Lay the king crab meat over two of the shokupan slices. Evenly spread the avocado mixture over the crab, then top with the remaining shokupan slices, mayo-side down.

5. Wrap in cling film (plastic wrap) and press in the fridge for 30 minutes.

6. To serve, trim the crusts and cut into squares.

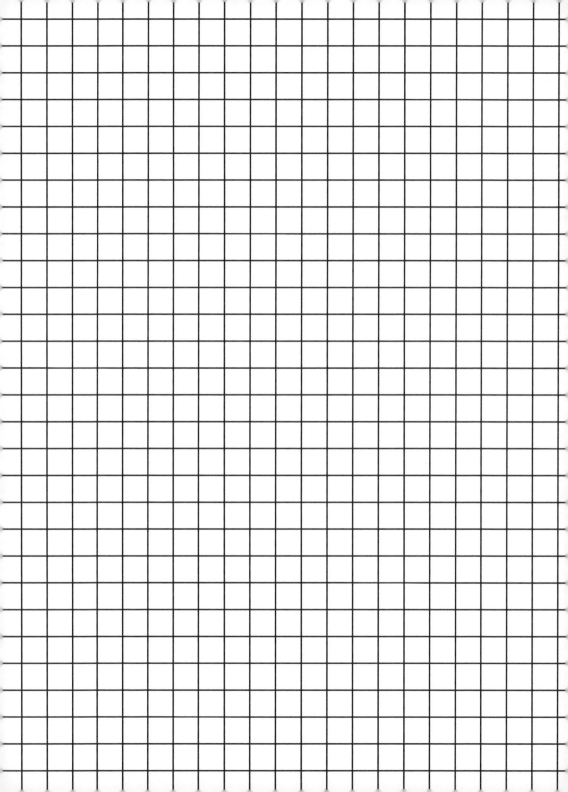

Meat

Mortadella Katsu with Mozzarella

モルタデッラカツとモッツァレラチーズ

This sando is like a spaghetti western filmed in Japan, featuring a mortadella katsu wrapped around a melting mozzarella centre.

Makes 2

32 thin slices mortadella (1 mm thick)
2 x 40 g (1½ oz) pieces firm mozzarella, each 6 x 5 cm (2½ x 2 in)
4 eggs, whisked
225 g (8 oz/1½ cups) plain (all-purpose) flour
200 g (7 oz/4 cups) dried panko
1 litre (34 fl oz/4 cups) rapeseed (canola) oil, for frying
4 tablespoons salted butter, softened
4 slices shokupan
125 ml (4 fl oz/1 cup) Tonkatsu Sauce (page 102)
2 teaspoons Shichimi Togarashi (page 97)

1. Layer the mortadella into four stacks of eight slices each. Place the mozzarella pieces on top of two of the stacks, in the centre. Using a small brush, egg-wash the mortadella stacks, then top each one with the remaining mortadella stacks, encasing the mozzarella inside.

2. As if you were making ravioli, press down to remove any air pockets (these could expand in fryer, splitting the stack). A toothpick through each corner (like a sewing pin) can help hold it all in place while you work.

3. From each mortadella and mozzarella stack, cut out a 9 x 10 cm (3½ x 4 in) rectangle. Lightly press again, and gently dust with flour, removing any excess. Dip in the egg-wash, ensuring full coverage to create a seal.

4. Coat in the panko, then repeat the egg-wash and crumb process once again. Gently pack down extra panko around the sides. Allow the stacks to sit in the panko for about 30 minutes to create a tight seal. Remove the toothpicks.

5. Place the oil in a deep-fryer and set to 160°C (320°F). Evenly spread the butter over four slices of shokupan.

6. Once the mortadella katsu have set, gently dust off any excess and slowly lower into the fryer. Cook for 4 minutes, flipping every minute to ensure an even fry.

7. Once golden brown, remove from the fryer and place on a wire rack to rest for about 4 minutes.

8. On a plate, combine the tonkatsu sauce with the shichimi togarashi.

9. Spread 1 tablespoon of the tonkatsu mixture on each slice of shokupan. Place the mortadella katsu on two shokupan slices and top with the remaining slices, tonkatsu-side down.

10. Press unwrapped (between two sheets of baking/parchment paper) for 10 minutes.

11. To serve, trim the crusts and cut widthways.

//

PREP/COOK TIME 50 minutes
PRESS TIME 10 minutes

Tempura Corn with Chicken-Skin Mayo

コーンのかき揚げ

What better complement for tempura corn than a chicken-skin mayo? Intense and crunchy, this sando could qualify as Japanese soul food.

Makes 2

2 whole corn cobs, husks and silk removed
1 tablespoon plain (all-purpose) flour
1 tablespoon cornflour (cornstarch)
60 g (2¼ oz/¼ cup) Tempura Batter (page 100)
½ teaspoon sea salt flakes
½ teaspoon curry powder
500 ml (17 fl oz/2 cups) rapeseed (canola) oil
6 tablespoons Roasted Chicken-Skin Mayo (page 95)
4 slices shokupan

1. Add the corn cobs to a pot of boiling water, and cook for 10 minutes. Once cooked, drain and set aside. Allow to cool to room temperature.

2. Cut the corn cobs in half widthways. Place cut-side down and cut off the kernels (you should have a total kernel weight of about 225 g/8 oz).

3. In a bowl, use your hand to lightly crush the kernels four times to release some of their juices.

4. Combine the plain flour and cornflour and sift into the corn kernels. Mix gently with a chopstick.

5. Add the tempura batter in a thin stream, a little at a time, ensuring the mixture is not too wet, because it will thicken. It should be bound together without any excess batter at the bottom of the bowl. Divide the mixture in half.

6. In a small bowl, combine the salt and curry powder and set aside.

7. In a medium frying pan (skillet), heat the oil to 150°C (300°F). Using a large spoon, gently lower one half of the tempura mixture into the

Meat

pan, keeping it intact. It should be approximately the same size as the shokupan slices.

8. Cook for 5 minutes, turning every minute. Remove and place on a wire rack to rest for 5 minutes. Repeat with the other half.

9. Meanwhile, evenly spread the roasted chicken-skin mayo over four slices of shokupan. Sprinkle the curry salt on both sides of the tempura pieces, then place on two of the slices of shokupan. Top with the remaining slices, mayo-side down.

10. Press unwrapped for 5 minutes.

11. To serve, trim the crusts and cut widthways.

//
PREP/COOK TIME 40 minutes
PRESS TIME 5 minutes

Chicken Karaage in Namban Sauce

南蛮ソース漬け チキン唐揚げ

Crispy fried chicken dressed
in a combination of sweet,
tangy *namban* and Japanese
tartare sauce.

Makes 2

60 ml (2 fl oz) Dashi Stock
   (page 89)
1 tablespoon Japanese mayo
1 tablespoon shoyu (soy sauce)
1 tablespoon sake
1 garlic clove, crushed
2 x 120 g (4¼ oz) chicken thighs
160 g (5½ oz/1 cup) cornflour
   (cornstarch)
40 g (1½ oz/¼ cup) plain
   (all-purpose) flour, plus
   1½ tablespoons
1 tablespoon potato starch
1 litre (34 fl oz/4 cups) vegetable
   oil
1 portion Japanese Tartare Sauce
   (page 91)
4 slices shokupan
1 portion Namban Sauce
   (page 93)

//
PREP/COOK TIME 45 minutes
PRESS TIME 10 minutes

1. Combine the dashi, mayo, shoyu,
sake, garlic and 1½ tablespoons
of the plain flour in a bowl and
mix thoroughly. Add the chicken
and marinate for 4–6 hours in a
container in the fridge.

2. In a medium-sized bowl, sift
together the cornflour, remaining
plain flour and potato starch.

3. Coat the marinated chicken in
this flour mixture. Once coated,
leave in the flour for 5 minutes.

4. Pour the oil into a heavy-based
pot off the heat. Place the pot
on the stove, then gently place
the chicken in the oil, trying to
avoid overlapping. Turn the heat
to medium–high. The chicken will
be ready when it is golden brown
and crisp, about 12–15 minutes.
Remove and rest on a wire rack for
15 minutes.

5. Evenly distribute the tartare
sauce across four slices of shokupan.

6. Dip the crispy chicken pieces
into the namban sauce on both
sides. Drip-drain and place two
of the shokupan slices.

7. Top with the remaining slices,
tartare-side down. Gently press,
unwrapped, for 10 minutes.

8. To serve, trim the crusts and cut
twice widthways.

Menchi Katsu

メンチカツ

Menchi is a Japanese term derived from the English word 'mince'. This yōshoku take on the hamburger is tasty enough to rival the original.

Makes 2

3 litres (104 fl oz/12 cups)
    rapeseed (canola) oil, for frying
1 tablespoon vegetable oil
¼ brown onion, peeled and diced
90 g (3¼ oz) fatty pork mince
    (ground pork)
140 g (5 oz) veal mince (ground
    veal)
3 eggs, 2 whisked
60 ml (2 fl oz) milk
140 g (5 oz/2⅓ cups) dried
    panko
salt and pepper
150 g (5 oz/1¼ cups) plain
    (all-purpose) flour
4 tablespoons tomato ketchup
1 tablespoon Worcestershire
    sauce
4 slices shokupan
100 g (3½ oz) white cabbage,
    shredded

1. Place the rapeseed oil in a deep-fryer and set to 170°C (340°F).

2. Heat the vegetable oil in a small pan over a medium heat. Once hot, add the onion and sweat for about 4 minutes until translucent. Set aside to cool to room temperature.

3. In a medium-sized bowl, combine the pork and veal mince, 1 egg, milk, 40 g (1½ oz/⅓ cup) of the panko and the sautéed onion. Season with salt and pepper to taste. (To test the seasoning, take a small amount and cook in a frying pan/skillet.)

4. Set up a crumbing station (page 12): in three consecutive trays, place the plain flour first, the whisked eggs second and the remaining 100 g (3½ oz/2 cups) panko third.

5. Divide the mince in half and shape into two 10 x 9 cm (4 x 3½ in) patties. Dust with flour, dip in the egg-wash and then fully coat in the panko, leaving no exposed areas.

6. Fry for 3 minutes, flipping every minute. Once ready, remove the menchi katsu from the fryer and place on a wire rack to rest for 5 minutes.

Meat

7. Combine the ketchup and Worcestershire sauce, then evenly spread ketchup mixture over four slices of shokupan.

8. Place the rested katsu on two of the shokupan slices. Divide the shredded cabbage and place over the katsu. Place the remaining shokupan slices on top, ketchup-side down.

9. Wrap in cling film (plastic wrap) and press for 10 minutes.

10. To serve, trim the crusts and cut widthways.

//

PREP/COOK TIME 45 minutes
PRESS TIME 10 minutes

Meat

Wagyu Short Rib Katsu with Karashi Mayo

This sando is lavish. Richly rendered Wagyu fat soaking into crispy nama panko, cut through with the bitter-radish flavour of mustard. It's a good time!

Makes 1

3 litres (104 fl oz/12 cups) rapeseed (canola) oil, for frying
180 g (6¼ oz) Wagyu short rib, bones removed, trimmed to 10 x 9 cm (4 x 3½ in)
225 g (8 oz/1½ cups) plain (all-purpose) flour
2 eggs, whisked
200 g (7 oz/3 cups) Nama Panko (page 12)
2 slices shokupan
1 portion Karashi Mayo (page 92)

//

PREP/COOK TIME 30 minutes
PRESS TIME 2 minutes

1. Place the oil in a deep-fryer and set to 170°C (340°F).

2. Meanwhile, bring the short rib to room temperature (don't skip this!).

3. Set up a crumbing station (page 12): in three consecutive trays, place the plain flour first, eggs second and nama panko third.

4. Dust the short rib with the flour, then dip in the egg-wash and fully coat in the panko, leaving no exposed areas.

5. Gently lower the short rib katsu into the fryer, trying to retain the crumb. Cook for 3 minutes for rare and 4 minutes for medium-rare, flipping every 30 seconds.

6. Once golden, place on a wire rack to drain for 4 minutes.

7. Toast one side of both slices of shokupan until golden brown. Place on a board, toasted-side down, and evenly spread the 1½ tablespoons of karashi mayo over each slice.

8. Once rested, place the short rib katsu on one slice and top with the remaining slice, mayo-side down.

9. Gently press between two pieces of baking paper (parchment) for 2 minutes.

10. To serve, trim the crusts and cut into thirds, widthways.

和牛ショートリブカツ 辛子マヨ

Ham Katsu with Yakisoba

ハムカツと焼きそば

This strange-but-delicious combination of layers brings a whole new meaning to the phrase 'comfort food'. Why choose one when you can have both?

Makes 2

3 litres (104 fl oz/12 cups) rapeseed (canola) oil, for frying
2 rashers streaky bacon, chopped
2 large shiitake mushrooms, stems removed, finely sliced
¼ brown onion, peeled and thinly sliced
40 g (1½ oz) sliced white cabbage
100 g (3½ oz) Japanese egg noodles, cooked
1 tablespoon sesame oil
3 tablespoons Tonkatsu Sauce (page 102)
75 g (2½ oz/½ cup) plain (all-purpose) flour
1 egg, whisked
75 g (2½ oz/1½ cup) dried panko
90 g (3¼ oz) ham, sliced 1 cm (½ in) thick and cut into 10 x 9 cm (4 x 3½ in) pieces
3 tablespoons salted butter, softened
6 slices shokupan

//

PREP/COOK TIME 60 minutes
PRESS TIME 20 minutes

1. Place the rapeseed oil in a deep-fryer and set to 180°C (350°C).

2. Start with the yakisoba. In a large frying pan (skillet) over a medium heat, combine the chopped bacon and mushrooms and stir for 2 minutes to render the fat. Add the sliced onion and cabbage, and cook for about 3 minutes until soft.

3. Add the cooked noodles and sauté, then add the sesame oil and tonkatsu sauce. Cook for a further 90 seconds, then set aside to cool.

4. Next, prepare the ham katsu. Set up a crumbing station (page 12): in three consecutive trays, place the plain flour first, egg second and panko third. Dust the ham in the flour, then dip in the egg-wash and fully coat in the panko. Rest in the crumbs for 5 minutes.

5. Place in a deep-fryer and cook for 2½ minutes until golden brown. Remove and place on a wire rack to drain for 5 minutes.

6. Spread the butter across six slices of shokupan. Divide the yakisoba over two slices. Top each yakisoba with another bread slice. Place the ham katsu on top and cover with the remaining slices of bread.

7. Wrap in cling film (plastic wrap) and press for 20 minutes. To serve, trim crusts and cut in half diagonally.

Meat

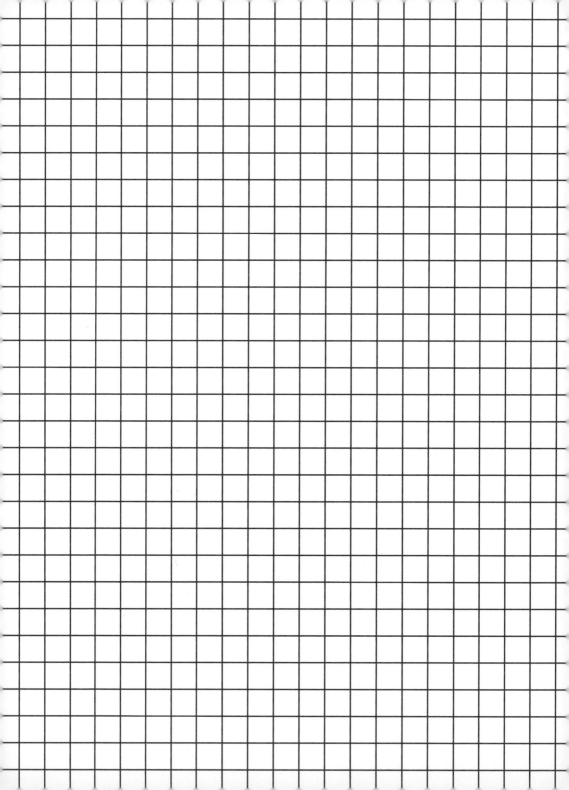

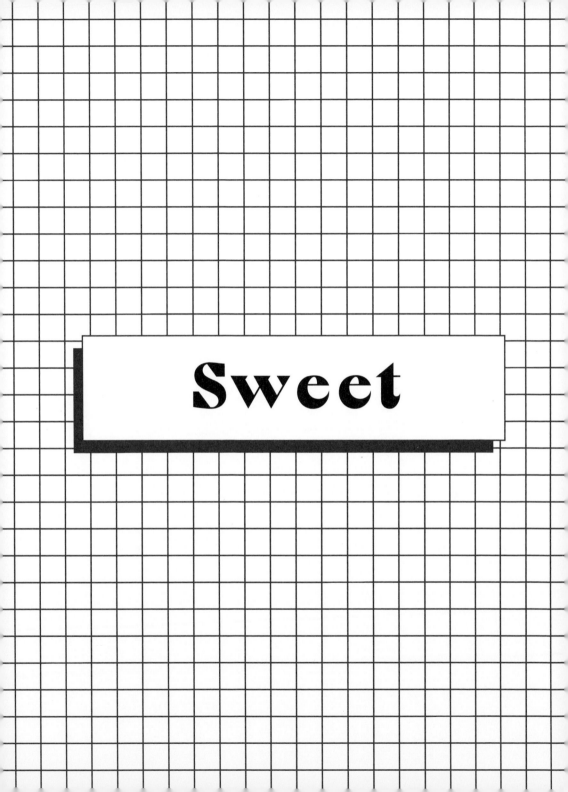

Sweet

Vanilla Coffee Ice Cream

バニラコーヒーアイス

This soon-to-be-classic recipe plays on the Japanese obsession with vanilla and coffee in a two-toned ice-cream sando.

Makes 2

4 slices shokupan

COFFEE ICE CREAM
120 ml (4 fl oz) whipping (thickened) cream
1 tablespoon glucose
1 tablespoon instant coffee
40 ml (1½ fl oz) skimmed condensed milk

VANILLA ICE CREAM
120 ml (4 fl oz) whipping (thickened) cream
1 tablespoon glucose
1 vanilla pod, scraped
40 ml (1½ fl oz) skimmed condensed milk

1. Grease and line a 20 x 12 cm (8 x 4½ in) loaf tin with cling film (plastic wrap).

2. For the coffee ice cream, place 40 ml (1½ fl oz) of the whipping cream and the glucose into a small saucepan over a medium–high heat and bring to a simmer for 60 seconds.

3. Remove from the heat, then add instant coffee and whisk for about 2 minutes until dissolved. Place the saucepan in a bowl of ice water until completely cool, stirring occasionally.

4. Combine the remaining whipping cream with the condensed milk and coffee mixture. Slowly whisk until soft peaks form. Pour evenly into the lined tin (give it a few light taps) and freeze for 40 minutes.

5. For the vanilla ice cream, combine 40 ml (1½ fl oz) of the whipping cream with the glucose and vanilla pods in a saucepan over a medium–high heat. Bring to a simmer for 60 seconds.

6. Remove from the heat and strain through a fine sieve. Place the saucepan in a bowl of ice water until completely cool, stirring occasionally.

7. Combine the remaining whipping cream with the condensed milk and vanilla mixture. Slowly whisk until soft peaks form. Pour evenly over the frozen coffee ice cream (give it a few light taps) and freeze for 3 hours.

8. To assemble, remove the layered ice cream from the tin and cut in half widthways. Place each piece in the centre of a slice of shokupan. Top with the remaining slices, then wrap in cling film (plastic wrap) and press for 1 hour in the freezer.

9. To serve, trim the crusts and cut in half.

//

PREP/COOK TIME 45 minutes
FREEZING TIME 4 hours
PRESS TIME 60 minutes

Sweet

Black Sesame Ice Cream with Red Bean

These flavours are as synonymous with Asian cooking as rice and soy sauce. Black sesame, with its earthy nuttiness, pairs beautifully with the smooth sweetness of red bean.

Makes 2

150 g (5½ oz/½ cup) red bean paste
4 slices shokupan

BLACK SESAME ICE CREAM
340 ml (11½ fl oz) whipping (thickened) cream
80 ml (2½ fl oz/⅔ cup) double cream
6 tablespoons glucose
75 g (2½ oz/⅔ cup) Sweet Black Sesame Paste (page 97)
100 ml (3½ fl oz) skimmed condensed milk

//
PREP/COOK TIME 60 minutes
FREEZING TIME 6 hours
PRESS TIME 60 minutes

1. Grease and line a 20 x 12 cm (8 x 4½ in) loaf tin with cling film (plastic wrap).

2. For the black sesame ice cream, combine 100 ml (3½ fl oz) of the whipping cream with the glucose and black sesame paste in a saucepan, over a medium–high heat. Bring to a simmer for 90 seconds, then set aside to cool completely.

3. Combine the remaining whipping cream, double cream and condensed milk with the cooled black sesame mixture. Slowly whisk until soft peaks form. Pour evenly into the lined tin (give it a few light taps). Freeze for 6 hours.

4. To assemble, spread the red bean paste evenly across four slices of shokupan.

5. Remove the ice cream from the tin and cut in half widthways. Place each piece on a slice of shokupan. Top with the remaining slices, bean paste-side down.

6. Wrap in cling film and press for 1 hour in the freezer.

7. To serve, trim the crusts and cut lengthways.

あずき 黒ゴマアイス

Mango and Yuzu Cream

マンゴーゆずクリーム

This is my take on the mango pancakes seen in Yum Cha/Dim Sum restaurants the world over. The yuzu cream's complex citrus profile matches the tropical sweetness of the mangoes perfectly.

Makes 2

3 tablespoons caster (superfine) sugar
6 teaspoons yuzu juice
120 ml (4 fl oz) whipping (thickened) cream
120 ml (4 fl oz) double (heavy) cream
4 slices shokupan
2 mango cheeks, peeled and each sliced into 4 pieces

//

PREP/COOK TIME 15 minutes
PRESS TIME 30 minutes

1. For the yuzu cream, combine the caster sugar and yuzu in a bowl and whisk until the sugar has dissolved.

2. Add the whipping cream and double cream to the yuzu juice, and whisk until medium–stiff peaks form.

3. To assemble, spread the yuzu cream evenly over four slices of shokupan, then divide the pieces of mango between two of the shokupan slices. Top with the remaining shokupan slices, cream-side down.

4. Wrap in cling film (plastic wrap) and press for 30 minutes in the fridge.

5. To serve, trim the crusts and cut into quarters.

Sweet

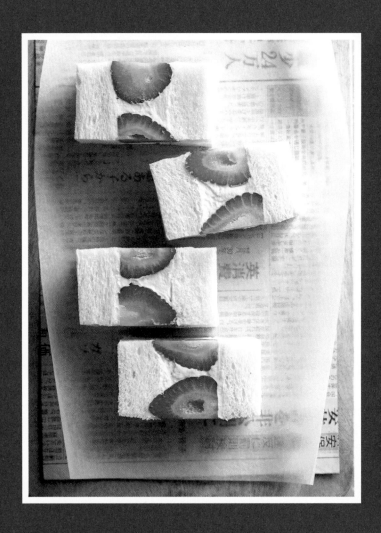

Strawberry and Sake Cream

This is a slightly boozier adaptation of a long-standing member of the sando family, with a delicate sake and strawberry perfume.

Makes 2

250 ml (8½ fl oz/1 cup) double (heavy) cream
3½ tablespoons caster (superfine) sugar
85 ml (3 fl oz) sake
18 strawberries
4 slices shokupan

//

PREP/COOK TIME 20 minutes
PRESS TIME 30 minutes

1. In a bowl, combine double cream, sugar and sake. Whisk until medium-stiff peaks form, being careful not to over-whip.

2. Wash the strawberries and pat dry on kitchen paper. Slice off the green tops, creating a flat surface.

3. Evenly spread the sake cream across four slices of shokupan. Lay the strawberries across two of the slices and top with the remaining slices, cream-side down.

4. Wrap in cling film (plastic wrap) and press for 30 minutes in the fridge.

5. To serve, trim the crusts and cut into four cubes.

イチゴ酒クリーム

Sweet Tamagoyaki in Citrus Sugar

甘たまご揚げサンド

This sando is actually a Korean street food. The sando is floured, egg-washed and fried until golden amber, then rolled in a citrus sugar. It's another great piece of creativity in the ever-evolving sando-verse.

Makes 2

1 litres (34 fl oz/4 cups) sunflower
  oil, for frying
2 eggs
80 g (3 oz/½ cup) cornflour
  (cornstarch)
50 g (1¾ oz/¼ cup) demerara
  sugar
zest of ½ orange
4 teaspoons salted butter,
  softened
4 slices shokupan
2 x 180 g (6¼ oz) Sweet
  Tamagoyaki, each trimmed into
  9 x 8 cm (3½ x 3 in) pieces
  (page 99)

//

PREP/COOK TIME 50 minutes
PRESS TIME 15 minutes

1. Place the oil in a deep-fryer and set to 160°C (320°F).

2. In a medium-sized bowl, whisk the eggs with 2 teaspoons of the cornflour until combined.

3. Add the remaining cornflour to a small tray.

4. In a separate baking tray (baking sheet), combine the sugar and orange zest and thoroughly mix.

5. Evenly spread the butter over four slices of shokupan. Lay the tamagoyaki pieces over two of the slices and top with the remaining slices, butter-side down.

6. Wrap in cling film (plastic wrap) and press for 15 minutes.

7. Unwrap and trim the crusts. Gently coat with cornflour and dust off any excess, then thoroughly coat in the egg-wash.

8. Gently place the sando in the fryer for 4 minutes, turning every minute.

9. Once golden brown, remove from the fryer and drain for a few seconds, then coat with the orange sugar, ensuring even coverage. Rest for 4 minutes.

10. To serve, cut into quarters and serve with extra orange sugar.

Sweet

Honeydew and Sweet Matcha Cream

メロンと抹茶クリーム

We couldn't have a Japanese cookbook without matcha! Matcha's bitter creaminess pairs perfectly with fruity honeydew. This is a fresh take that will impress even those who aren't fans of melon.

Makes 2

4 tablespoons Sweet Matcha
  Cream (page 98)
4 slices shokupan
7 slices honeydew melon, seeds
  and rind removed

//

PREP/COOK TIME 15 minutes
PRESS TIME 30 minutes

1. Spread 1 tablespoon of the matcha cream on each slice of shokupan.

2. Layer the slices of honeydew melon evenly over two of the slices of shokupan, overlapping them slightly. Top with the remaining shokupan slices, matcha cream-side down.

3. Wrap in cling film (plastic wrap) and press for 30 minutes in the fridge.

4. To serve, trim the crusts and cut in half.

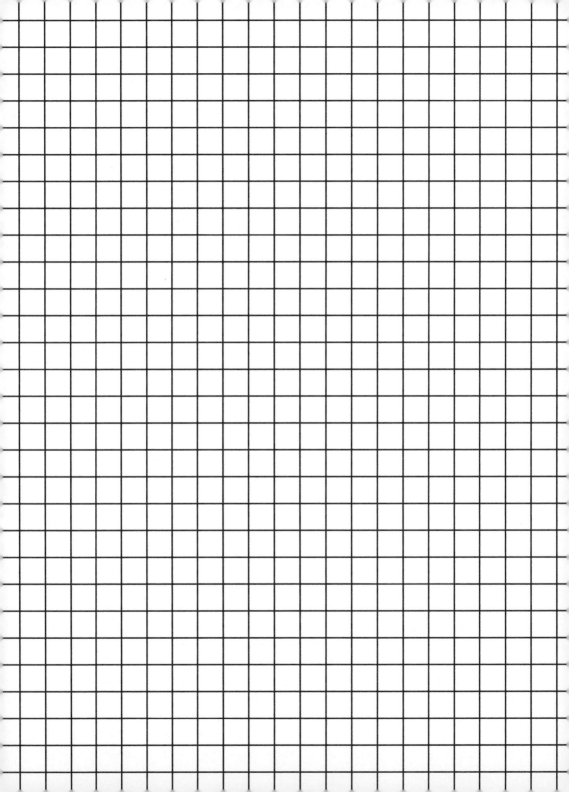

Basics

Chicken Liver Pâté

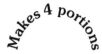 Makes 4 portions

450 g (1 lb) chicken livers, cleaned
500 ml (17 fl oz/2 cups) full-fat
  (whole) milk
½ small brown onion, peeled and
  thinly sliced
1 garlic clove, crushed
½ teaspoon fresh thyme leaves
125 ml (4 fl oz/½ cup) water
salt and pepper
40 ml (1½ fl oz) cognac or brandy
165 g (5¾ oz) unsalted butter,
  at room temperature, chopped

1. Soak the livers in the milk for 6 hours in a container in the fridge.

2. Strain and pat the livers dry. In a medium pan over a medium heat, combine the livers, onion, garlic, thyme, water and a pinch of salt. Sweat off for 5 minutes, being sure not to overcook the livers, because that will make the pâté grainy.

3. Add the cognac or brandy and cook for a further 30 seconds.

4. Transfer the mixture to a high-speed food processor and blitz on high for 90 seconds, or until smooth.

5. With the food processor still on, add the butter, 1 tablespoon at a time, until completely emulsified.

6. Place the mixture in a small container with cling film (plastic wrap) covering the surface of the pâté, then leave in the fridge for 6 hours to set.

7. Remove the cling film before serving.

Dashi Stock

Makes 850 ml

1 piece dashi kombu, cut into a
   15 x 5 cm (6 x 2 in) rectangle
1 litre (34 fl oz/4 cups) water
35 g (1 oz) bonito flakes

1. With a damp cloth, wipe away any white residue from the kombu.

2. Place the water into a medium-sized pot. Add the kombu and allow to sit, off the heat, for 30 minutes.

3. Now place the pot over a medium heat and bring the soaked kombu and water to 85°C (185°F). Do not boil or the stock will become bitter, much like over-steeping tea.

4. Using a spoon, skim any foam that comes to the surface, then remove the kombu and add the bonito flakes. Turn off the heat and allow the mixture to steep for 10 minutes.

5. Place a muslin cloth over a fine strainer and sieve the stock.

6. Leave the stock to cool and store in an airtight container. This will keep for up to 3 days in the fridge.

Dashimaki Tamagoyaki

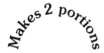

6 eggs
220 ml (7½ fl oz) Dashi Stock
  (page 89)
1 teaspoon caster (superfine)
  sugar
1 tablespoon shoyu (soy sauce)
rapeseed (canola) oil, for frying

1. In a medium-sized bowl, combine the eggs, dashi, sugar and soy. Whisk together using chopsticks. Pass through a fine sieve.

2. Place a 22 cm (8½ in) tamago pan over a medium-high heat and lightly grease with rapeseed oil by folding a small piece of kitchen paper into a 4 x 2 cm (1½ x ¾ in) rectangle and dipping it into the oil, then sweeping it around the pan.

3. Pour in a thin layer of the egg mixture, adding just enough to cover the bottom of the pan. Pop any air bubbles. Once the bottom of the omelette begins to set, roll the omelette towards yourself.

4. Once rolled, push the omlette to the front of the pan. Lightly grease the back half of the pan with more rapeseed oil.

5. Repeat with another thin layer of egg mixture, gently lifting the bottom of the already cooked omelette to bind the two together. Pop any air bubbles.

6. Starting at the front of the pan, roll the omelette on top of itself. Repeat this process until all the mixture is used up. Between each roll, remember to press the rolled omelette against the edge of the pan to give it a rectangular shape.

7. Gently place the finished tamago on a piece of cling film (plastic wrap). Gently wrap and place in fridge to chill, ready for later use. This will keep for up to 1 week in the fridge, or can be frozen for up to 3 months.

Basics

Japanese Tartare Sauce

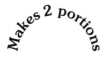

Makes 2 portions

½ white onion, peeled and finely diced

½ cucumber, seeds removed, finely diced

2 hardboiled eggs, halved and yolks separated

60 ml (2 fl oz) Japanese mayo

½ tablespoon rice vinegar

½ tablespoon tomato ketchup

salt and pepper

1. Soak the diced onion in lukewarm water for 30 minutes.

2. Finely mince the boiled egg whites and add to a bowl. Add the cucumber, then gently crumble in the egg yolks.

3. Add the mayo, rice vinegar and ketchup.

4. Once soaked, strain the onion. Place onto kitchen paper and squeeze dry, then add to the bowl with the other ingredients.

5. Mix to combine, then season to taste with salt and pepper.

6. This will keep in an airtight container in the fridge for up to 2 days.

Karashi Mayo

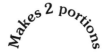

Makes 2 portions

250 ml (8½ fl oz/1 cup) Japanese
  mayo
2½ tablespoons karashi mustard
1 teaspoon crushed Japanese
  pepper

1. Place all the ingredients in a bowl and stir thoroughly to combine.

2. Store in an airtight container with cling film (plastic wrap) across the top until required. This prevents a skin forming. This will keep for up to 2 days in the fridge.

Miso Butter

Makes 2 portions

100 g (3½ oz) unsalted butter,
  softened
40 g (1½ oz) shiro miso paste
1 teaspoon sesame oil

1. Ensure the butter is soft enough to whip. Combine the butter, shiro miso and sesame oil in a bowl, then whip until fully combined.

2. If using immediately do not place in the fridge as it will solidify and you will need it soft to spread. When storing for later use place in the fridge.

3. This will keep for up to 2 days.

Miso Glaze

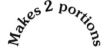

Makes 2 portions

1 teaspoon shoyu (soy sauce)
1 teaspoon mirin
1 teaspoon rice vinegar
1 tablespoon caster (superfine)
  sugar
1½ teaspoons shiro miso paste
1 teaspoon sesame oil
1 teaspoon sake

1. In a small saucepan over a low heat, combine the shoyu, mirin, rice vinegar and sugar. Stir for about 30 seconds until the sugar has dissolved.

2. Remove from the heat and add the miso paste. Stir until fully combined, then add the sesame oil and sake.

3. Set aside until ready to use. This will keep for up to 5 days in an airtight container in the fridge.

Namban Sauce

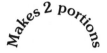

Makes 2 portions

2 tablespoons shoyu (soy sauce)
2 tablespoons caster (superfine)
  sugar
3 tablespoons rice vinegar

1. In a small saucepan over a low heat, combine the shoyu and sugar. Whisk for about 30 seconds until the sugar has dissolved.

2. Remove from the heat and place in a small bowl, then stir in the rice vinegar.

3. Cool and set aside for later use. This will keep for up to 1 week in the fridge.

Ponzu

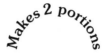

Makes 6 portions

150 ml (5 fl oz) sake
150 ml (5 fl oz) mirin
300 ml (10 fl oz) shoyu
10 g (¼ oz) dashi kombu
12 g (½ oz) bonito flakes
150 ml (5 fl oz) rice vinegar
200 ml (7 fl oz) orange juice
200 ml (7 fl oz) lemon juice
100 ml (3½ fl oz) yuzu juice

1. Combine the sake and mirin in a medium-sized pan over a high heat. Bring to the boil, then stand back and carefully set alight to burn off the alcohol: this will take about 30 seconds.

2. Pour into a medium-sized bowl. Add the remaining ingredients and stir until combined. Cool over an ice bath.

3. Store in an airtight container for 1 week before use (it will keep for up to 3 weeks).

Ponzu Butter

Makes 2 portions

zest of ½ lemon
170 g (6 oz) unsalted butter,
  at room temperature
60 ml (2 fl oz) Ponzu (see left)

1. In a small bowl, whisk together the lemon zest and butter. This will help release some of the oils in the zest.

2. Slowly add the ponzu until completely combined.

3. Set aside in a cool place for later use. This will keep for up to 2 days in the fridge.

Basics

Roasted Chicken-Skin Mayo

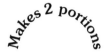

Makes 2 portions

120 g (4¼ oz) chicken skin,
  roughly chopped
2 egg yolks
2 teaspoons rice vinegar
4 tablespoons rapeseed (canola)
  oil
salt and pepper

1. Preheat the oven to 160°C (320°F/ gas 4) and line a baking tray (baking sheet) with baking (parchment) paper.

2. Scrape any excess fat from the back of the chicken skin, then evenly disperse the skin over the tray, making sure it is lying flat. Roast for about 40 minutes until golden brown, removing any pieces that start to burn.

3. Once crisp, place the skin on kitchen paper and allow to cool for 10 minutes.

4. Place in a small high-speed blender and blitz until it forms a fine crumb. Add the egg yolks and vinegar, then blitz for a further 30 seconds.

5. With the blender still on, pour in the rapeseed oil in a thin stream until emulsified. Season with salt and pepper to taste. (The mayo should be thick and taste of roasted chicken skin.)

6. To store, place a small piece of cling film (plastic wrap) directly on top of the mayo to prevent a skin forming. This will keep for up to 3 days in the fridge.

Roasted Prawn Oil

Makes 10 portions

250 ml (9 fl oz) rapeseed (canola)
  oil
130 g (4½ oz) ebi prawn (shrimp)
  shells
2 tablespoons tomato purée
  (paste)
1 small shallot, peeled and
  roughly chopped
2 garlic cloves, bruised, skin on
1 small celery stalk, roughly
  chopped
1 fresh bay leaf
½ teaspoon sea salt flakes

1. Heat 4 tablespoons of rapeseed oil in a medium-sized saucepan over a high heat. Once the oil is smoking, add the prawn shells and salt, then stir for about 4 minutes until the shells become toasted and aromatic.

2. Add the tomato purée and stir for 1 minute.

3. Add the shallot, garlic, celery and bay leaf, then reduce the heat to low and sweat for 4 minutes. Be sure to scrape any residue from the bottom of the pan to avoid burning.

4. Add the remaining oil and heat on low for about 90 minutes. Take off the heat and allow to infuse for a further 120 minutes.

5. Once infused, strain through a fine sieve and lightly press out any excess liquid from the shells.

6. This will keep for 1 week in an airtight container in the fridge.

Shichimi Togarashi

Sweet Black Sesame Paste

Makes 4 portions

Makes 1 portion

4 tablespoons white sesame seeds,
lightly toasted
4 teaspoons cayenne pepper
1 teaspoon ground ginger
½ teaspoon white pepper
2½ tablespoons dried mandarin
peel, ground
1 nori sheet, toasted (page 12)

160 g (5¾ oz/1 cup) black sesame
seeds
2 tablespoons pure honey

1. Combine all the ingredients
(except the nori) in a medium-sized
bowl.

2. Tear the nori sheet into a
high-speed blender and blitz to form
fine flakes. Add to the bowl with the
other ingredients and stir. Store in
an airtight container. This can last
for up to 3 weeks but will lose its
complexity of flavour.

1. Toast the sesame seeds in a
medium-sized frying pan (skillet)
over a low–medium heat, stirring
continuously, until aromatic.

2. While still warm, place in a
high-speed food processor with
the honey. Blitz until completely
smooth.

3. Place in an airtight container
with a layer of cling film (plastic
wrap) over the surface to prevent
a skin forming. This will keep for
up to 1 month in the fridge if stored
correctly.

Sweet Matcha Cream

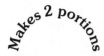

Makes 2 portions

125 ml (4 fl oz/½ cup) whipping
(thickened) cream
1½ tablespoons caster
(superfine) sugar
1 tablespoon matcha powder
125 ml (4 fl oz/½ cup) double
(heavy) cream

1. Combine the whipping cream and sugar in a medium-sized bowl, then sift in the matcha powder. Stir in gently so as not to over-whip. Mix until the matcha and sugar are well incorporated.

2. Add the double cream and whip until soft peaks form.

3. To store, place a piece of cling film (plastic wrap) directly on top of the matcha cream and cover completely. Set aside in fridge for up to 30 minutes until ready to use.

Sweet Tamagoyaki

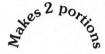

Makes 2 portions

100 ml (3½ fl oz) water
1 tablespoon caster (superfine)
  sugar
2 teaspoons mirin
pinch of salt
6 large eggs
3 tablespoons rapeseed (canola)
  oil

1. Combine the water, sugar, mirin and salt in a small bowl, then whisk for about 2 minutes until the sugar has dissolved. In a separate bowl, whisk the eggs with chopsticks to avoid over-aerating, then pour in the mirin mixture and whisk until combined.

2. Place a 22 cm (8½ in) tamago pan over a medium–high heat and lightly grease with rapeseed oil by folding a small piece of kitchen paper into a 4 x 2 cm (1½ x ¾ in) rectangle and dipping into the oil, then sweeping it over the pan.

3. Pour in a thin layer of the egg mixture, just enough to cover the bottom of the pan. Pop any air bubbles. Once the bottom of the omelette begins to set, roll the omelette towards yourself.

4. Once rolled, push the omelette to the front of the pan. Lightly grease the back half of the pan with more rapeseed oil.

5. Repeat with another thin layer of egg mixture, gently lifting the bottom of the already cooked omelette to bind the two together. Pop any air bubbles. Starting at the front of the pan, roll the omelette on top of itself. Repeat the process until all the mixture is used up. Between each roll, remember to press the rolled omelette against the edge of the pan to give it a rectangular shape.

6. Gently place the finished tamago onto a piece of cling film (plastic wrap). Gently wrap and place in the fridge to chill, ready for later use. This will keep for up to 3 days.

Tempura Batter

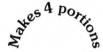
Makes 4 portions

75g (2½ oz/½ cup) plain
(all-purpose) flour
80 g (3 oz/½ cup) cornflour
(cornstarch)
2 egg yolks
300 ml (10 fl oz/1¼ cups)
ice-cold water

1. In a medium-sized bowl,
sift together the plain flour and
cornflour. Make a well in the centre.

2. Into the well, place the egg yolks
and 60 ml (2 fl oz) water. Whisk with
chopsticks, slowly bringing the flour
into the centre to make a paste.

3. Continue to add water until the
batter is sufficiently mixed and no
large lumps remain.

4. Set aside in a cool place until
ready to use.

Tentsuyu

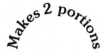
Makes 2 portions

100 ml (3½ fl oz) Dashi Stock
(page 89)
25 ml (1 fl oz) shoyu (soy sauce)
25 ml (1 fl oz) mirin

1. In a small saucepan, combine the
dashi, shoyu and mirin, and bring to
the boil over a medium heat.

2. Once boiled, remove from the
heat and use immediately, or store
in an airtight container and serve
cold at a later time. This will keep
for up to 1 week in the fridge.

Toasted Nori Mayo

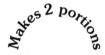

Makes 2 portions

1 sheet nori, toasted (page 12)
125 ml (4 fl oz/½ cup) Japanese
  mayo
½ teaspoon sesame oil

1. Tear the toasted nori into small pieces and place in a blender. Blitz on high for about 90 seconds until it resembles a fine powder.

2. In a small bowl, combine the mayo, sesame oil and powdered nori. Whisk together until completely combined.

3. To store, place a small piece of cling film (plastic wrap) directly on top of the mayo to prevent a skin forming. Store in a cool place, ready for later use. This will keep for up to 1 week in the fridge.

Tonkatsu Sauce

Makes 700 ml

200 g (7 oz/1 cup) caster
  (superfine) sugar
60 ml (2 fl oz) water
100 ml (3½ fl oz) red wine
1 brown onion, peeled and
  roughly chopped
1 carrot, peeled and roughly
chopped
1 apple, peeled, cored and roughly
  chopped
6 large ox heart tomatoes,
  roughly diced
6 prunes
1 tablespoon tomato purée
  (paste)
2 whole cloves
1 fresh bay leaf
½ teaspoon ground nutmeg
125 ml (4 fl oz/½ cup) shoyu
  (soy sauce)
60 ml (2 fl oz/¼ cup) rice vinegar
3 tablespoons Worcestershire
  sauce
1 tablespoon dark soy sauce

1. Heat the sugar and water in a large pot over a medium heat and cook for about 3 minutes until it becomes a dark caramel.

2. Add the red wine and stir to stop the caramel from darkening further. Add the onion, carrot, apple, tomatoes, prunes and remaining water. Simmer for 5 minutes.

3. Add the tomato purée, cloves, bay leaf, nutmeg, shoyu, rice vinegar, Worcestershire sauce and dark soy, then cover with a lid and simmer for a further 30 minutes.

4. Remove the whole spices and transfer the mixture into a high-speed blender. Blitz on high for 2 minutes (or until completely smooth), then pass through a fine sieve. Thin out with a little water if desired.

5. Cool before storing in the fridge in an airtight container until required. This will keep for up to 1 month.

Tsuyu Glaze

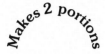

Makes 2 portions

500 ml (17 fl oz/2 cups) Dashi
  Stock (page 89)
4 tablespoons mirin
1 tablespoon caster (superfine)
  sugar
4 tablespoons shoyu (soy sauce)
1 tablespoon cornflour
  (cornstarch)
½ teaspoon salt

1. Combine the dashi, mirin and sugar in a medium-sized saucepan over a medium heat. Add all but 1 teaspoon of the shoyu and bring to the boil.

2. Once boiled, set aside and remove 125 ml (4 fl oz/½ cup) of the liquid, placing it in a small bowl. Add the cornflour to the bowl and whisk to create a slurry (making sure there are no lumps).

3. Pour the slurry back into the pan with the remaining sauce and stir over a medium heat for 2 minutes. Taste to ensure the cornflour is completely cooked. (The sauce should resemble a light caramel.)

4. Once cool, add the remaining teaspoon of shoyu and set aside for later use. This will keep for up to 2 days in the fridge.

Basics

Wasabi Cream Cheese

Makes 2 portions

1½ tablespoons good-quality
  wasabi
1 teaspoon rice vinegar
120 g (4¼ oz) cream cheese,
  at room temperature
2 tablespoons sour cream
salt and pepper

1. Combine the wasabi and rice vinegar in a small bowl.

2. In a separate bowl, gently whip together the cream cheese and sour cream until soft peaks form.

3. Fold the cream cheese mixture into the wasabi mixture, being careful not to over-whip. Season with salt and pepper to taste. This will keep for up to 2 days in the fridge.

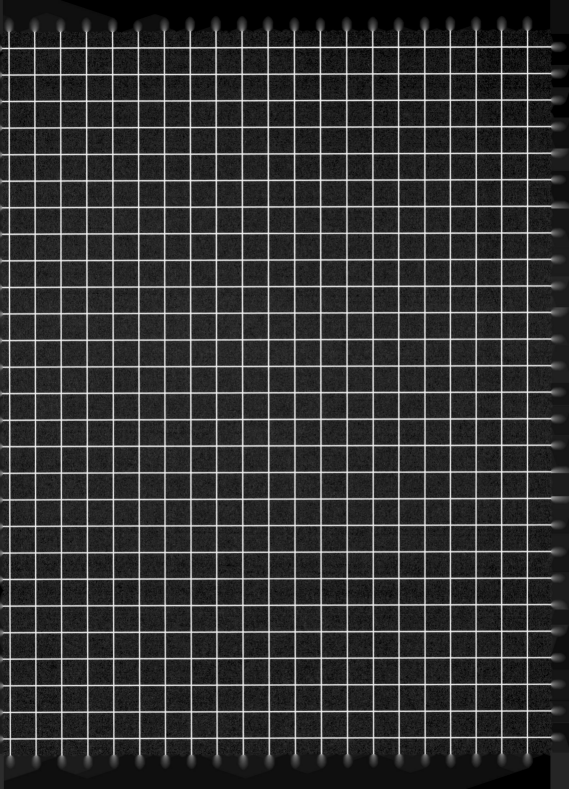

Index

索引

Index

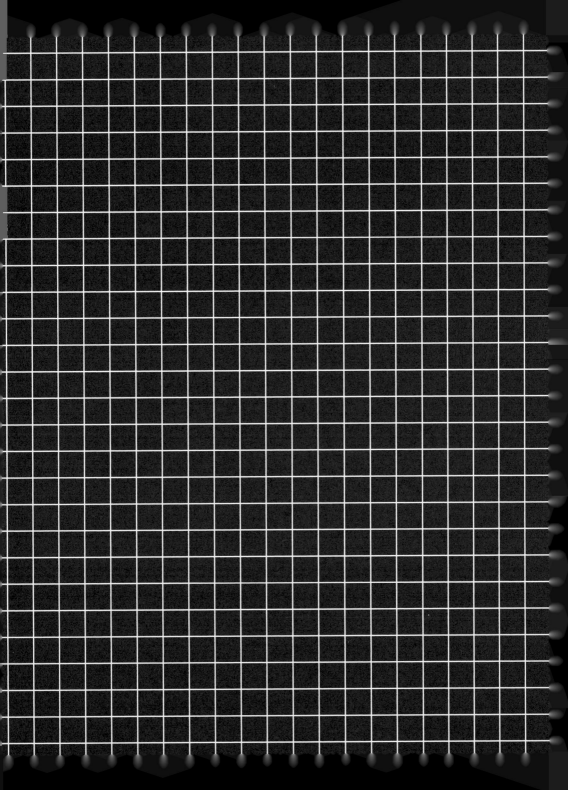

Acknowledgements

あとがき

Firstly, I would like to thank my publisher, Mark Campbell. Not only for the opportunity to write my first cookbook, but also for the collaborative spirit you've brought to the entire project. To have been able to work with such creative freedom has been an absolute dream.

Alan Benson: generous, kind and a master of puns. When it comes to your work, you always seem to find the light spot (eye roll, haha!). You're a dear friend — thank you for all your guidance.

To Vanessa Austin, for the joy you bring to every shoot and your meticulous eye for beauty and composition. For going above and beyond what was asked, I adore you and am eternally grateful.

To Jess Cox, for your fastidious editing, and Mietta Yans, for having the hardest job of making me look cool with your magnificent design powers.

To my assistant, John, thank you for every shopping trip and for answering every last-minute text without a single complaint. Thanks also to chef Kenji Maenaka for your time and generosity towards my many questions.

Finally, to my partner, Ryan, thank you for your immeasurable support and patience. Be it as stenographer while I rant recipes at you in the kitchen into the late hours of the night, or as official sando taste-tester while I study your face after each bite. You're always there and I'll never take it for granted. I love you.

First published in 2023 by HarperCollins Publishers Australia Pty Limited.
This Hardie Grant edition is published by arrangement with HarperCollins
Publishers Australia Pty Limited. This edition published in 2023 by Hardie Grant
Books, an imprint of Hardie Grant Publishing.

Hardie Grant Books (London)
5th & 6th Floors
52–54 Southwark Street
London SE1 1UN

Hardie Grant Books (Melbourne)
Building 1, 658 Church Street
Richmond, Victoria 3121

hardiegrantbooks.com

British Library Cataloguing-in-Publication Data. A catalogue record for this book
is available from the British Library.

Cult Sando
ISBN: 978-1-78488-602-8
10 9 8 7 6 5 4 3 2 1

For the HarperCollins edition:
Japanese proofreader: Hanna Imai
Designer: Mietta Yans, HarperCollins Design Studio
Photographer: Alan Benson
Stylist: Vanessa Austin

For the Hardie Grant edition:
Publishing Director: Kajal Mistry
Acting Publishing Director: Emma Hopkin
Commissioning Editor: Kate Burkett
Senior Editor: Eila Purvis
Proofreader: Tara O'Sullivan
Production Controller: Stephen Lang

Colour reproduction by p2d
Printed and bound in China by Leo Paper Products Ltd.

Jimmy Callaway has worked as a professional chef for over fifteen years at some of Sydney's top restaurants, including the Four in Hand Dining Room, Oscillate Wildly and Firedoor.

After leaving Firedoor, he pursued a food pilgrimage to Europe and settled in Emilia-Romagna, a region in the north of Italy, where he lived above a restaurant, learned to make pasta and educated himself on the Italians' uncompromising passion for regionality and produce.

Through travel, Jimmy has gained a passion for understanding people and culture through the lens of food. He also works as a freelance recipe developer and food writer for publications like *Gourmet Traveller*, and in food production for television. *Cult Sando* is his first cookbook.

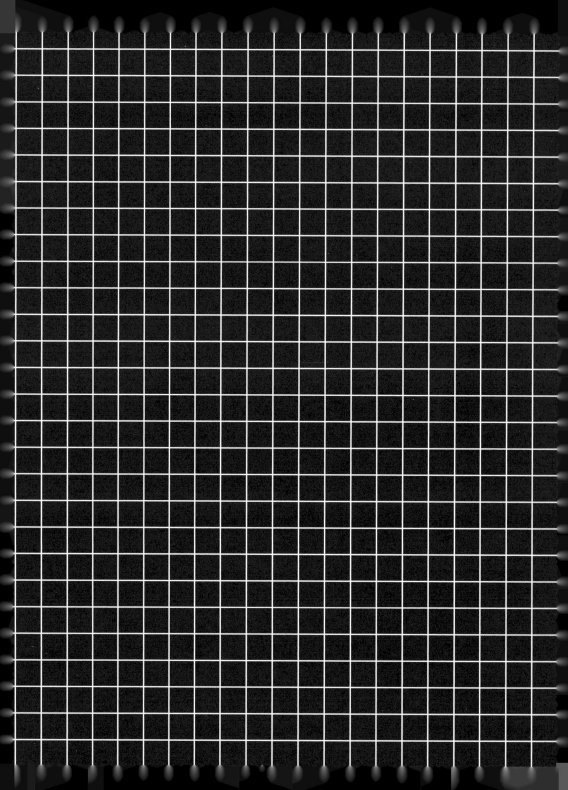